# Industry, Expansion and Empire: Britain 1750–1900

STEVE BUXTON

# Acknowledgements

Mary Evans Picture Library p.5 bottom, p.18 top left, pp.28-29, p.37 left; The Science Museum/Science & Society Picture Library p.8, p.11 left; British Waterways p.9; The Science Museum/TheBridgeman Art Library p.11 top right; The Hulton-Deutsch Collection p.11 bottom right, p.18 top right, p.37 right; E.T. Archive p.12, p.41 top right; Image Select p. 13 top; The Billie Love Historical Collection p.13 bottom; Manchester Public Libraries p.16; BEAMISH The North of England Open Air Museum p.18 bottom left, p.22; H.P. Merton/Robert Harding Picture Library p.20 left; Ironbridge Gorge Museum Trust p.21; Bristol City Council p.24; The Maritime Trust p.25 left; The Illustrated London News Picture Library p.25 right; The Mansell Collection p.26 left and right, p.34 right, p.39; Courtesy of the Director, National Army Museum, London p.29; British Library/The Bridgeman Art Library p.33; MuseumAfrica p.34 left; Yale University Art Gallery, Trumbull Collection p.35; Topham Picturepoint p.41 left; private collection/The Bridgeman Art Library p.42 left; Manchester City Art Galleries p.42 right.

For Joanne and Victoria

British Library Cataloguing in Publication Data
Buxton, Steve
    Industry, Expansion and Empire: Britain 1750–1900 (Action History Series; Vol. 4)
    I. Title II. Series
    000.00

    ISBN 0 340 60279 1

First published 1995
Impression number    10  9  8  7  6  5  4  3  2  1
Year                       1999  1998  1997  1996  1995

Typeset by Litho Link Ltd, Welshpool, Powys.
Printed in Great Britain for Hodder & Stoughton Educational, a division of Hodder Headline Plc, 338 Euston Road, London NW1 3BH by Cambus Litho, East Kilbride

# Contents

# 1

# *Changing Britain*

**industry, factory, energy, statistics, increase, population, decrease**

There were great changes in Britain between 1750 and 1900. These changes affected nearly everyone. People invented new ways of making things and better ways of moving things around the country. The first factories were built and small towns grew into large 'industrial' cities.

1760 Jane Hughes is my name. When I was a girl I lived in a country village. To earn a living my family made cloth. We all used to work together in our cottage.

1795 When I was fifteen my parents moved to this town to find work. Now I have a family of my own. My husband is a coal miner. Me and the children work in the factory. The factory makes cloth much faster and cheaper than we used to at home in the old days.

**Source A** A Black Country town in 1869

## TALKING POINTS

1   Why do you think people like Jane Hughes moved to a town to live?

2   Look at Source A on the previous page. What sorts of energy are being used in the picture? What different sources of energy do we use today? Make a list of those which you use that are not shown in the picture.

3   Do you think industrial towns were healthy places to live? Why/why not?

## WORKFILE

One way we can learn more about the past is by looking at 'statistics'. The time 1750–1900 was one of great change. What can we learn about these changes from statistics?

Look at Source B. Copy and complete the following question and answers. Choose the correct word from the words in the brackets.

1   How did the population of Britain change in this period?

The population (increased, decreased).

b   The population (increased, decreased) most between (1750 and 1800,  1800 and 1850, 1850 and 1900).

c   The population (increased, decreased) least between (1750 and 1800,  1800 and 1850, 1850 and 1900).

**Source B**   Population of Britain

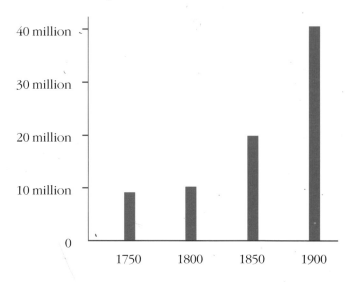

2   Look at Source C. Copy and complete the following question and answers. Choose the correct word/words from those in the brackets.

**Source C**   Populations living in towns and cities

= percentage of population living in towns and cities.

a   In 1800 (a few, many) more people lived in (the countryside, towns and cities).
b   In 1850 (a few, many) more people lived in (the countryside, towns and cities).
c   In 1900 (a few, many) more people lived in (the countryside, towns and cities).

3  Look at Source D below. It shows how many thousands of people lived in four British cities. How did the population of cities change? Copy the sentences that follow and complete them in your own words.

a  The population in all four cities . . . .
b  The city whose population changed the most was . . . .
c  The population of this city in 1900 was about . . . times bigger than it had been in 1750.
d  The city whose population changed the least was . . . .

**Source D**  Table showing population growth

| City/town | 1750 | 1900 |
|---|---|---|
| Liverpool | 35 thousand | 704 thousand |
| Glasgow | 24 thousand | 776 thousand |
| Norwich | 35 thousand | 80 thousand |
| Birmingham | 25 thousand | 523 thousand |

**Source E**  Towns with more than 100,000 people

4  In 1800 London and Dublin were the only British cities where more than 100,000 people lived. By 1900 the picture had changed as you can tell by looking at Source E.
"Source E shows that only a few parts of the country were affected by a growing population." Do you agree with this statement? Write a few sentences to say why you agree or disagree.

PUTTING IT ALL TOGETHER
5  We have learned a lot about the way Britain changed by looking at statistics. Use Table 1 to sum up what you have found out. Copy it out. Put a tick by each statement. Tick the **T** column if you think the statement is true. Tick the **F** column if you think it is false. The last box in the table is blank. Add a statement of your own.

**Table 1**

| Statements | T | F |
|---|---|---|
| Very few factories were built between 1750 and 1900. | | |
| The population of some cities grew enormously. | | |
| The population changed more in some areas than in others. | | |
| People moved from towns to the countryside to find work. | | |
| In 1850 the environment was cleaner than today. | | |
| | | |

# 2 *Why Did Britain Change?*

## New Machinery

What caused Britain to change so much between 1750 and 1900? There were many reasons. New ways of making things were discovered. New machines were invented. People used them in factories. New ways were found to transport people and goods.

## Clothmaking

Clothmaking had always been one of Britain's most important industries. In the 18th century several new machines were invented to speed up clothmaking. The machine in the picture is called the 'Mule' (Source A). It was invented by Samuel Crompton in 1779.

## Steam and Iron

New and better steam engines were made by James Watt after 1776. You can find out more about these on page 11.

In 1709 Abraham Darby found new ways to make a lot of cheap iron. Iron was a very important material. Engines, bridges, rails and many more things were made from iron. Darby's company built the world's first iron bridge in 1779.

**Source A** Crompton's mule This machine speeded up the spinning of cotton. Samuel Crompton designed it for using in homes and it was only later that it was put to use in factories.

## Factories

Factories were built for the first time. There were lots of machines and workers together in one building. One of the first factories was opened by Richard Arkwright in 1771. You can find out more about him on pages 14 and 15.

## Canals and Railways

Canals and railways were built. Now heavy goods could be moved cheaply and easily. The Duke of Bridgewater built one of the first canals, opened in 1761. Source B shows cargo boats on a canal in London.

The first public railway ran from Stockton to Darlington and was opened in 1825. A few years later in 1830 Britain's first major railway was opened. This linked Liverpool and Manchester.

### WORKFILE

**1** Look at the boxes on page 10. Fill in the missing words on your copy. Choose from these words:

machines    steam    transport    links    factories    method

**2** Use your boxes to complete the timeline. Use the dates on the timeline to help you decide where to put them.

**3** Draw a line from each box to the correct point on the timeline.

**Source B** The Regent's Canal, London

| Richard Arkwright opens one of Britain's first . . . . . . . . . . . . . . making cotton thread. | Duke of Bridgewater's canal proves to be a great way to . . . . . . . . heavy goods. | Britain's first public railway . . . . . . . . . . . . . . the towns of Stockton and Darlington. |
| --- | --- | --- |
| Boulton and Watt produce new . . . . . . . . . . . . . . engines. | Abraham Darby tries a new . . . . . . . . . . . . . . for iron making. | The Mule was one of several new . . . . . . . . . . . . . . used to make cloth. |

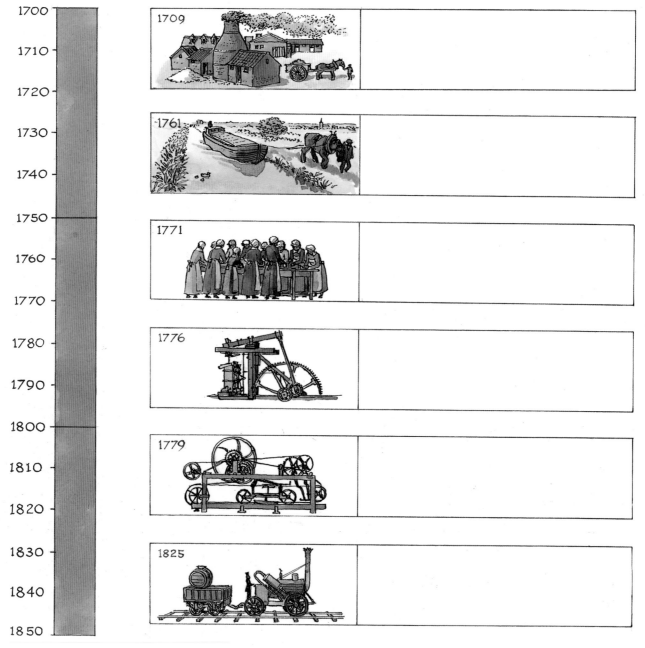

# Steam Power Causes Change

The first steam engines were used in the early 1700s. Sometimes they were called 'fire' engines. Fire provided heat to boil water and make steam. By 1788 the firm of Boulton and Watt were making very useful steam engines at their factory in Birmingham.

## Boulton and Watt

James Watt was an inventor. William Murdoch was the factory foreman. He helped Watt improve the design of the old-fashioned steam engines. Watt's engines were very powerful and could turn a wheel (Source C).

Matthew Boulton set about selling the new engine. He said to one visitor to his factory: 'I sell here, Sir, what all the world desires to have, power'.

Source C  Watt's steam engine

### TALKING POINTS

**1** Look at Source D. There are two steam engines in this picture. What jobs do you think they are doing?

# Steam Power. What Were the Results?

Over the next 50 years this new power affected people's lives in all sorts of ways. Thousands of engines were made. They provided power for factories and mines (Source D). Engines were used to pull trains on the new railways (Source F on the next page). Some farmers used them too (Source E). Even fairgrounds used them to power rides. Wherever power was needed in the 19th century you could usually find a steam engine.

Source D  A colliery near Leeds

Source E  Threshing using steam power

**2** Look at Source E. How is the power from the engine driving the threshing machine? What do you think the machine does?

**Source F**  The St Helens and Runcorn Gap
Railway

**3**  Look at Source F. How many steam engines are at work in this picture?

**4**  What forms of power are used most today? Make a list. Which ones are better for our environment than steam? Why/why not?

**WORKFILE**

**1**  Imagine you have just visited Boulton and Watt's factory in 1788. Suppose Boulton showed you around. He introduced you to Watt and Murdoch. Write a letter to a friend. Tell them:

**a**  who you met and what they said

**b**  what sort of new machine you have seen (you might try to draw it)

**c**  why you think these machines are going to become very popular.

**2**  Make a list to show the uses of steam power.

**3**  Use your list to help you draw a diagram called 'What was steam power used for in the 19th century?'.

**4**  Design a machine of your own which could be run on steam power. Make a drawing with labels. Say what your invention is called and describe what it will be used for.

# 3

# *Changing the Way Goods Were Made*

spinning, weaving, handloom,
bankrupt, profit

## *Making Cloth*

Clothmaking takes place in several stages. The main stages are spinning and weaving (Source A).

In 1700 thread and cloth was usually made in people's houses. It was very hard work. Everyone in the family joined in. Women and girls usually did the spinning on a spinning wheel (Source B). Men did the weaving using a handloom. Scenes like those in Source C could be found in cottages all over the country.

**Source A**

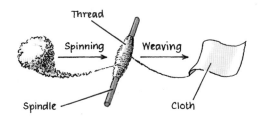

### TALKING POINTS

1 Look at a piece of cloth you are wearing. See how the thread has been woven into cloth. In 1700 most cloth was made from woollen thread.

a What sort of materials are our clothes made from these days? Make a list.

b Which materials are most popular now?

c Which ones would not have been available in 1700? Why?

**Source B** Spinning at home

**Source C** Weaving at home

# Sir Richard Arkwright

By 1850 clothmaking at home had almost vanished. There were thousands of textile factories instead. Why did this change happen? One of the first factories was built by a businessman named Richard Arkwright (Source D). He often worked from 5 o'clock in the morning till 9 o'clock at night. Someone who knew him said: 'His mind was as coarse as it was bold and active, his manners rough and unpleasing'. What can we learn from his story?

**Source D**

What a success it was. People started calling my machines Water frames. We had rooms full of them at Cromford.

Now there's spinning factories all over England. I own a lot of 'em myself of course. That's why I'm so rich. Can't stop here all day talking. There's work to be done.

## WORKFILE

1 Imagine you are a reporter in Cromford in 1771. A new factory opens in the town today. You are sent to report the event. Make up a headline. Write your report. Try to:

a describe the new factory. What does it make? How big is it? What machines are used there?

b Interview Mr Arkwright, the owner. What sort of a man is he? What has he done in the past? What does he say about his new factory?

c Interview local hand spinners. Are they pleased about the new factory? Why? Why not?

# Factory Owner

Play this game and see if you could have made it as a factory owner in 1780.

**You will need:**
- a die or numbered papers
- three to five players
- a copy of the 'account sheet' on page 17 for each player.

## Aim

You are a rich person with five thousand pounds in the bank (a lot of money in 1780). Make up a name for yourself and write it on your 'accounts sheet'. You aim to buy textile factories. Each factory will cost you one thousand pounds. If you buy wisely the factories will make you even more money. Bad luck and bad buys can bankrupt you. The winner is the person who has made the most money by the end of the game.

## How to play

**Round one, 1780**

1 Each person decides how many factories to buy. You can buy five or you could buy less and leave some money in the bank. Fill in your decision in column one on your account sheet.

2 Throw the die. Use the events chart on page 17 to see what happens to your factory. Write what happens to you in column two on your account sheet.

3 Work out how much money you have made or lost. Write it in column three in your account sheet (profit and loss).

4 Work out how much money you have got left in your bank account. Write it in column four of your account sheet.

5 Repeat steps one to four for each round. At the start of each round you can sell factories as well as buy them for £1000 each.

## Bankrupt

In bad years you could go bankrupt if you loose more money than you have in the bank. (The value of your factories doesn't count.) If you go bankrupt you can take no further part in the game until the end. At the end you can sell your factories for the usual price so you are still in with a chance of winning.

## Winning the Game

At the end of round five (1784) everyone sells their factories for £1000 each. Add the money to any you already have in the bank. The winner is the person with the most money.

**Source E**

The inside of a cotton factory

## Accounts sheet

| | Start of round | What happened? | Profit/loss | Total at end of year |
|---|---|---|---|---|
| **Round 1** 1780 | No. of factories owned <br> - - - - - - - - - - <br> £ in bank | | | No. of factories owned <br> - - - - - - - - - - <br> £ in bank |
| **Round 2** 1781 | No. of factories owned <br> - - - - - - - - - - <br> £ in bank | | | No. of factories owned <br> - - - - - - - - - - <br> £ in bank |
| **Round 3** 1782 | No. of factories owned <br> - - - - - - - - - - <br> £ in bank | | | No. of factories owned <br> - - - - - - - - - - <br> £ in bank |
| **Round 4** 1783 | No. of factories owned <br> - - - - - - - - - - <br> £ in bank | | | No. of factories owned <br> - - - - - - - - - - <br> £ in bank |
| **Round 5** 1784 | No. of factories owned <br> - - - - - - - - - - <br> £ in bank | | | No. of factories owned <br> - - - - - - - - - - <br> £ in bank |

## Events chart

| No. on die | What happened | |
|---|---|---|
| 1 | Average year. Thread sells well. | Make £2 000 for each factory owned. |
| 2 | Bad year. Factory workers strike. | Lose £1 000 for each factory owned. |
| 3 | Very good year. Install new, faster machines. | Make £4 000 for each factory owned. |
| 4 | Average year. Thread sells well. | Make £2 000 for each factory owned. |
| 5 | Bad year. Lack of power/dry river. | Lose £1 000 for each factory owned. |
| 6 | Good year. Sell thread to foreign countries. | Make £3 000 for each factory owned. |

# Factory Towns

technology, **mechanical, energy**

By 1900 there were thousands of factories in Britain. Near each factory houses were built for the factory workers. Towns grew into cities as more factories and houses were built. Source F shows what one factory town, Bradford, looked like by 1870. By this time most factories used steam engines to drive their machines. You can see their chimneys in the picture.

**Source F**

**Source G**  Unloading coal at the pit head

**Source H**  An engineering works

## TALKING POINTS

 In the nineteenth century not everyone worked in a cotton factory though. There were many other important industries. Sources G and H show two examples.

1  Try to find out which industries were important in your area in the 19th century.

2  Look at Sources G and H. For each one try to work out:
a  what is being produced
b  what skills the workers would need in order to do their jobs.

# Technology in Action

New technology was an important part of Britain's Industrial Revolution.

- New machines were invented to make things faster and cheaper than ever before
- Mechanical power took over as steam engines improved
- More coal was dug from the ground. Burning coal provided heat energy, energy to boil water, to drive steam engines and trains, energy to fire furnaces and kilns to make iron and pottery
- New ways were found to make iron and steel for machines and tools

## WORKFILE

1 Draw and fill in the diagram to show how technology was important in the Industrial Revolution. Complete the sentences in the boxes. Add a sentence or two of your own in each box. Improve your diagram with one or two drawings.

2 Write a sentence or two in your own words to answer these questions.

a Why did towns and cities grow where there were factories?

b Why was coal so important during the Industrial Revolution?

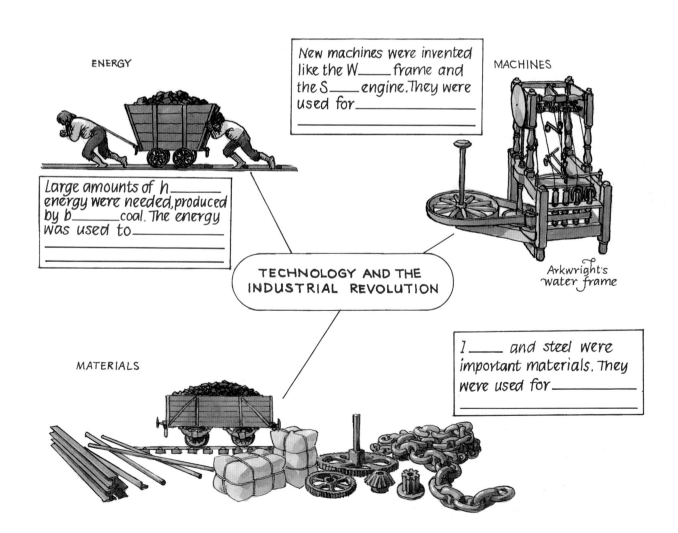

ENERGY

New machines were invented like the W____ frame and the S____ engine. They were used for____

MACHINES

Large amounts of h____ energy were needed, produced by b____ coal. The energy was used to____

TECHNOLOGY AND THE INDUSTRIAL REVOLUTION

Arkwright's water frame

MATERIALS

I____ and steel were important materials. They were used for____

# 4 Britain and World Trade

## import, export, transport, competition

Many of the things we use in our lives are not made or grown in Britain. Many cars, microwaves, videos and foodstuffs are imported from other countries. Britain also sells or exports goods to other countries. This worldwide trade needs modern forms of transport to carry goods over long distances (Source A).

Source A  A container ship being unloaded

## TALKING POINTS

1  A new video recorder is made in a factory in Japan. What forms of transport might be used to bring it to the shops near you?

2  Make a list of as many imported goods as you can.

3  What sort of goods do you think Britain exports today? Make a list.

4  Look at Source B below. It shows which imports and exports were common in 1750. Look at your lists. Tick any things which would also have been imported and exported in 1750.

Source B  Imports and exports to Britain, 1750

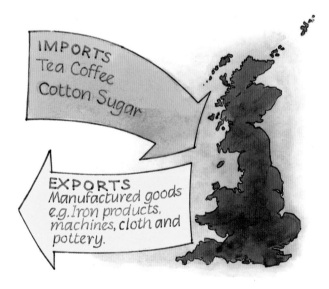

IMPORTS
Tea Coffee
Cotton Sugar

EXPORTS
Manufactured goods
e.g. Iron products,
machines, cloth and
pottery.

## WORKFILE

1  Write a sentence about each of the following words. Explain what they mean.

export     import     transport

2  Draw a diagram called 'Imports and Exports to Britain Now'. Use Source B as a guide. Use the information from your lists to write in the details.

# The Workshop of The World

In the 1700s there was a smaller amount of world trade than today, but it was growing. Britain was a manufacturing country, one of the main ones in the world. Factories and workshops here made lots of things which could be sold abroad. They made things like cloth, machines, engines, pottery and iron goods.

Look at Source C below. These items were made out of cast iron by the Coalbrookdale company. They were sold to customers in Africa, the USA and Australia. One of the fountains was bought by the government of Chile in South America.

This trade made a lot of money for British companies and plenty of jobs for British workers. By 1850 some people called Britain 'The workshop of the world'. However by 1900 Britain faced competition from other countries like Germany and the USA. They were making more goods than Britain and selling them at cheaper prices.

## WORKFILE

1 Suppose you work for the Coalbrookdale company in 1850. You have received an order from the Tsar (*king*) of Russia. He wants three grand iron fountains for the front of his palace. It is your job to design them. People in Victorian times loved very 'ornate' shapes. Draw your designs. Write a sentence or two to describe their main features.

2 Write a paragraph about 'Britain, workshop of the world'.

3 Choose any two present-day items which would not have been imported in 1750. Write a short paragraph to explain why these items would not have been imported in 1750.

4 In 1750 Britain imported tea and coffee. Write a sentence to explain why we still need to import tea and coffee more than 200 years later.

5 In 1750 Britain imported lots of raw cotton. Write a sentence to say what you think it was used for.

**Source C** Iron fountains made in Britain

# Which Goods Did Britain Import?

More goods from abroad were being sold in Britain too. In 1700 many imported items were expensive. By 1900 everyone could enjoy the benefits of imported goods. The shelves in local shops were packed with food grown abroad.

Source D shows a co-op shop around 1900. It has been re-created in a museum. The first co-op opened in Rochdale in 1844. The shop aimed to sell goods at fair prices to working people. Soon, all over the country, shops like co-ops were selling imported foods as well as British goods.

## TALKING POINTS

1 There are many museums like Beamish who try to re-create the past. How do you think visiting these museums helps people understand history better?

2 "Source D is a new picture. The shop was re-created in 1985 so it does not give us a true picture of the past." Do you agree or disagree with this statement. Why? Why not?

## WORKFILE

1 Study Source D carefully. Look at the items on the shelves. Match the numbers with Table A below to help you identify the items. Write in the names of the items on your copy of Source E.

| Table A | |
|---|---|
| **1** Currants | **5** Sugar |
| **2** Sultanas | **6** Wheat cereal |
| **3** Cocoa | **7** Coffee |
| **4** Semolina | |

2 Use Table B to work out which part of the world each item came from. Finish your copy of Source E by writing in where each item came from. Sometimes items may come from more than one place.

3 Look at Source E and your copy of Source F. Draw a line to link each item and the part of the world it came from.

**Table B**

| Imports | Source of supply |
|---|---|
| Cocoa | West Indies<br>South America<br>Philippines |
| Coffee | South America/Africa |
| Currants | Greece |
| Semolina | Russia |
| Sugar | West Indies |
| Sultanas | USA |
| Wheat cereal | USA |

**Source D** A co-op shop re-created at the Beamish Museum

C·W·S·PELAW BOOT POLISH

**Source E**

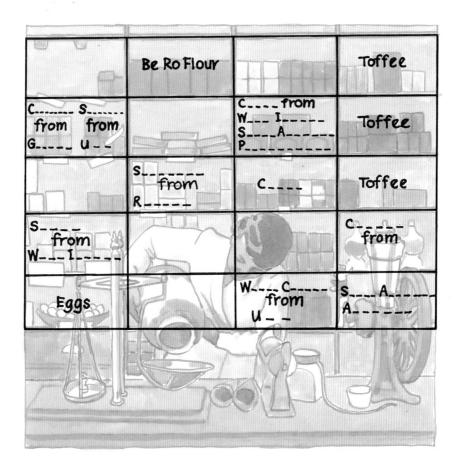

| | Be Ro Flour | | Toffee |
|---|---|---|---|
| C_____ S_____ from from G_____ U__ | | C____ from W___ I_____ S____ A_____ P_____ | Toffee |
| | S_____ from R_____ | C____ | Toffee |
| S_____ from W__I_____ | | | C_____ from |
| Eggs | W____ C_____ from U__ | | S___ A_____ A_____ |

**Source F**  Map of imports

*Industry, Expansion and Empire* © Steve Buxton. Published by Hodder and Stoughton.

# 5

# "Moving the Goods"

## warehouse, bale, barrel

Carrying goods by sea has always been important to Britain's trade with other countries. Before aeroplanes were invented all our trade had to pass through sea ports. Goods made in Britain were taken from the factory to the nearest port. They were loaded on ships and sent to other parts of the world. These goods are called exports. Ships coming to Britain carried goods called imports. Their goods were unloaded and stored in warehouses near the dockside before being sold.

Source A shows what a port would have looked like around 1700. Over the next 200 years ports like London, Glasgow, Bristol and Liverpool became even more important as Britain's trade grew.

## WORKFILE

1 Imagine you went to Bristol docks in 1720 looking for work. One of the merchants gave you a job for a day working on the quayside. Write a letter to your parents. Tell them:
- who you met during the day
- what sort of things you were asked to do
- what was going on around you
- how you felt at the end of the day after you got paid

Use these words to help you:
sailing ships    crane    packhorse
bale    barrel    merchant    warehouse

It might help if you look at Source A and try to imagine you are one of the people shown in the picture.

Source A  Bristol docks in 1720

# How Did Ships Change?

## Source B  The *Cutty Sark*

Sailing ships improved between 1750 and 1900. 'Clipper' ships like the *Cutty Sark* were built to go faster and hold more cargo (Source B).

After 1800 some ships were driven using steam engines. At first steam ships were used close to the coast in case they broke down. As their design became better they were used more and more on ocean crossings. Isambard Kingdom Brunel designed steamships to cross the Atlantic Ocean. The biggest was the *Great Eastern* launched in 1858. It caused quite a stir when it arrived in the USA (see Source C). Many other large steamships were in use by 1900 though there were also still many sailing ships.

## TALKING POINTS

1  Look at Source C. Find the paddles that drove the ship through the water and the other paddle steamer in the picture.

2  How does the size of the *Great Eastern* compare to the sailing ships in Source C?

3  Think about the docks in Source A. Docks like these could not handle ships like the *Great Eastern*. How would the docks and warehouses have to change?

## Source C  The *Great Eastern*

## WORKFILE

1  Suppose you work for the *Illustrated New York Times* in 1860. You have been sent to cover the arrival of the *Great Eastern*. Write your report. Draw a picture to help your readers imagine the event.

2  Study Table A below. Draw a bar graph to show how Britain's trade grew between 1700 and 1850. Use a different colour for exports and imports.

Table A

|  | Exports | Imports |
|---|---|---|
| 1700 | £7 million | £6 million |
| 1800 | £35 million | £26 million |
| 1850 | £145 million | £74 million |

3  Write a sentence or two to say what the graph is showing.

# 6

# India. A Closer Look at Trade

## First Traders

In 1600 the East India Company was formed in London by a group of merchants. They planned to send ships to far–off places like India to trade. They would return to Britain with silks, jewels and spices to sell (Source A).

**Source A** The start of the East India company

The first expedition, led by Captain Hawkins, reached India in 1608. Hawkins went to the emperor's palace at Delhi where he got permission to set up a trading post and warehouse. The company began trading with Indian merchants. Soon cargoes of goods were regularly being sent back to Britain. Over the next 50 years many more trading posts were set up. They became known as 'factories'. They were very different from British factories as you can see from Source B.

**Source B** An East India Company factory

## TALKING POINTS

1 Look at Source A. What event is shown here? When did it happen?

2 The people in Source A are making a hard decision. What do you think some of the main people might be saying?

3 Source B was a trading post in India. Compare it with the picture of Bristol docks you saw on page 24. How are the two scenes similar? How are they different? Look at what people are doing and how they are dressed.

## WORKFILE

1 Write a sentence or two about each of the following:

a The East India Company

b goods from India

c factories in India.

# What Was India Like?

Traders from the East India Company were among the first British visitors to India. They had little idea what to expect. This game will show you some of the things they discovered about India.

**How to play**

You will need:

- three or four players
- die or numbered papers.

It is 1700. Your ship is anchored in Bombay. Each round of the game you leave the ship to discover something new about India. Take it in turns to throw the die to find out where to go. You might go to some places more than once. Go back to the ship at the end of each round. Write an entry for the ship's log to say what you have found out. The winner is the first person to visit all six places.

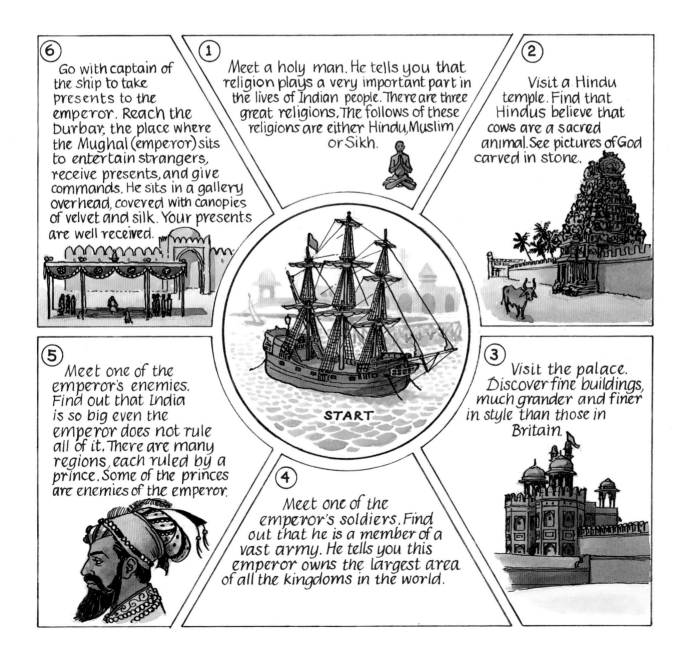

**6** Go with captain of the ship to take presents to the emperor. Reach the Durbar, the place where the Mughal (emperor) sits to entertain strangers, receive presents, and give commands. He sits in a gallery overhead, covered with canopies of velvet and silk. Your presents are well received.

**1** Meet a holy man. He tells you that religion plays a very important part in the lives of Indian people. There are three great religions. The follows of these religions are either Hindu, Muslim or Sikh.

**2** Visit a Hindu temple. Find that Hindus believe that cows are a sacred animal. See pictures of God carved in stone.

**5** Meet one of the emperor's enemies. Find out that India is so big even the emperor does not rule all of it. There are many regions, each ruled by a prince. Some of the princes are enemies of the emperor.

**4** Meet one of the emperor's soldiers. Find out that he is a member of a vast army. He tells you this emperor owns the largest area of all the kingdoms in the world.

**3** Visit the palace. Discover fine buildings, much grander and finer in style than those in Britain.

START

# How Was Trading Made Safe?

**sepoy, regiments, culture**

In the 18th century trade increased. More and more ships made the trip from Britain to India and back. The ships became known as 'East Indiamen'. The journey was not easy. You can see from Source C how far the ships had to travel.

The sailors were at sea for months at a time. They braved terrible storms and scorching heat. Sometimes the ships were attacked by pirates. Some ships never made it back to Britain. Most did make it though and the Company became very rich.

**Source C**

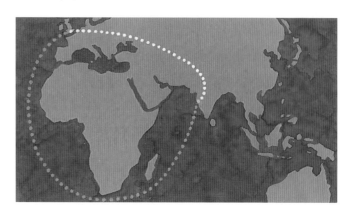

## Company Soldiers

The factories in India also had to be protected. Bands of robbers sometimes attacked traders or stole goods from the warehouses. At different times Britain was at war with other European countries like France. Their ships and soldiers attacked the British factories.

**Source D**  The Company harbour and factory at Bombay

The Company had its own soldiers. Some were British, but most were Indians. They were called sepoys. As trade increased the Company army grew bigger. Source E shows three of their soldiers. They were well armed and well trained. Their uniforms were similar to British army uniforms at that time. By 1700 they were a very powerful force.

**Source E** Soldiers of the Company army

Some Indians were happy with this. They made money from their trade with Britain. Other Indians though resented the way the British seemed to be taking over part of their land.

## WORKFILE

**1** Look at Source D. Copy and complete this table. Match the items with the correct numbers from Source D.

| Feature | Number |
|---|---|
| East Indiamen | |
| Warehouse | |
| Company Crest | |
| Harbour | |
| Fortress | |
| English Church | |

**2** Copy and complete this paragraph. Use these words: traders    India    long    the    forts    stations

In the 1700s and 1800s trading with . . . was a dangerous business. Ships had to travel . . . distances. They had cannons to defend themselves . . . . East India Company set up many trading . . . . They were called factories. The company built . . . . and employed soldiers to protect the . . . .

## TALKING POINTS

**1** 'The evidence proves that the British in India did not copy the Indian way of life. Instead they followed their own traditions and culture.'

Look at the evidence on the last 4 pages. Do you agree or disagree with this statement?

# How Did British Power Spread?

**viceroy**

Between 1700 and 1900 British power and influence spread all over India. When Emperor Aurangzeb died in 1707 rulers from different parts of India fought wars against each other. Some rulers were friendly with the British. The Company used their soldiers to help these princes win battles. In return the prince allowed the Company to expand trade in his area.

In time the Company's armies became the most powerful force in India. They fought battles against any Indian ruler who stood in their way. In this way the Company came to control large areas of India. No Indian prince could rule without their help.

The Company had come to India to trade. It did not do a very good job of ruling. In 1857 the British government took over. They sent a viceroy to govern all India.

Many Indians though did not accept the British as their rulers. By 1947 they had forced the British to leave India. The picture strip below shows some of the main events in the story.

## TALKING POINTS

(Read the picture strip first.)

**1** The British took over when the Indian rulers became weaker. What happened to make them weaker?

**2** What evidence is there that some Indians did not accept the British as their rulers?

**3** One British survivor of the Black Hole of Calcutta said that 124 people died there. Modern Indian historians disagree. They say 43 people died. Who do you think is right? Why?

An Indian prince named Suraj al Dowlah throws some British people into a small cell in Calcutta. The next morning only 22 people are alive in the 'Black Hole'. Some British people demand revenge.

British commander, Robert Clive is sent to India. He uses company soldiers to defeat Suraj's army at the Battle of Plassey. Many of Suraj's cannons do not work because his gunpowder gets damp in the rain.

The British take over Delhi, capital of the Moghul Empire. The emperor is allowed to carry on ruling, but only if he does what the British tell him.

Rebellion spreads across India as some sepoys refuse to obey orders from the British officers. The British, helped by friendly sepoys, defeat the rebels after bitter fighting.

After the rebellion the East India Company is closed down, and the British government takes over the rule of India. The British queen, Victoria, takes on the title 'Empress of India'.

Ghandi leads peaceful protests against British rule. Millions of Indians refuse to cooperate with the British. The British leave India and the Indians set up their own government.

## WORKFILE

1 Study Source F. Find out when and where each of the events you have read about took place by matching the numbers with the picture strip on pages 30 and 31. Write out the numbers, dates and places from the map with the captions from the picture strip.

2 Use this information to make your own timeline of events.
● Plan your timeline by using those you made before as an example (see page 10)
● You have to cover the period 1600–1945. How many years is this? How long will your timeline be?

● Write your own information boxes for your timeline.
● Add these two events. You read about them on page 26. You will need to look up the dates 'The East India Company is formed.' 'First British trading ships arrive in India.'

3 Draw a map to show where these events happened.

4 Work with a partner. Choose one of the events from the picture strip (on pages 30 and 31). Suppose you were a newspaper reporter at that time. Write a report about the event. Make up a good headline. One of you should write the report from an Indian point of view and one from a British point of view. Think about how the two reporters might say different things.

Source F Events in Britain and India

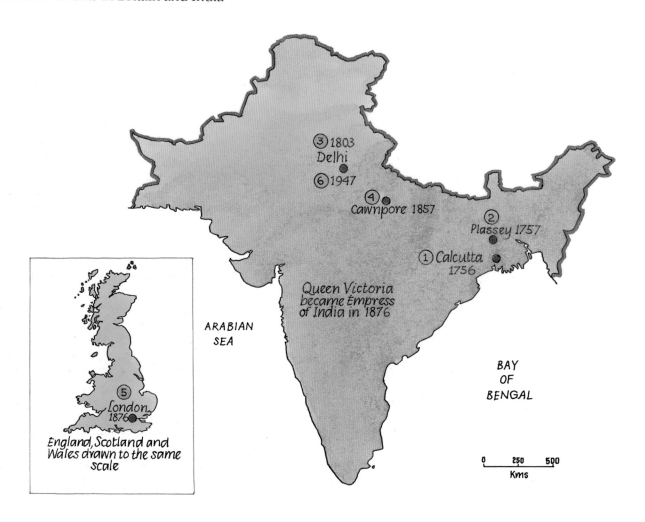

# 7

# The British Empire

**empire, colony, native, exploit, slave, independent**

We have seen how the British set out to trade with India and in the end became rulers of the whole country. During the same period of time Britain came to rule many other areas of the world. The map on the inside front cover of this book shows the many countries of the British Empire. As in India, the British army and navy often had to fight wars to win and keep control of these places, which were known as British colonies.

## Why Did the Empire Expand?

There were many reasons why Britain took control over other parts of the world. Trade was one very important reason. Other places produced valuable goods as well as India. South Africa produced gold and diamonds. The West Indies produced sugar (Source A).

**Source A** Cutting sugar cane

When Britain took control of these places British traders could fix prices to suit themselves. They made a lot of money. The Empire was certainly good for them.

In the 19th century Europeans explored parts of Africa for the first time. They claimed the land for their empires even though there were people living there already (Source B).

**Source B** A meeting between European soldiers and Africans

Britain claimed some places just to stop other European countries having them. For example, they did not want them to fall into French or German hands.

Some countries in the Empire were very different to India and Africa. There were smaller numbers of people already living there. Many British people went to live in places like North America and Australia to escape harsh conditions at home. Before long there were more British people living there than natives.

Most British people at the time were proud of the Empire. They felt that having a big empire proved that Britain was the best, most important country in the world.

# Was the Empire Good for the Colonies?

The Empire was not run for the benefit of the colonies. British traders often exploited the land and the people they controlled. The worst example of exploitation was the slave trade. Thousands of people were taken from Africa to the West Indies in British slave ships (Source C).

## Slavery

British traders owned sugar cane fields in the West Indies. They bought slaves and made them work in the sugar plantations (Source A on page 33).

**Source C** Slaves being taken on board ship

Some British people knew slavery was wrong. William Wilberforce led a group of protestors in London. They managed to get laws passed that banned the slave ships. The government put an end to slavery all over the Empire in 1833.

In some ways the Empire helped the people in the colonies. British machines and inventions were used around the Empire. The British built railroads in Africa and India that benefited everybody.

# How did Colonies Become Independent?

By 1776 those people who had settled in the North American colonies did not like being ruled from London. They said they would leave the Empire. They declared independence. The British sent a large army to stop them. The war which followed lasted for six years. The Americans won and forced the British to leave. They started a new country, the United States of America. Britain still controlled the part of North America called Canada.

Most other colonies though did not gain their independence until the middle of the 20th century. By then things had changed. Britain's army and navy was no longer so powerful. The views of many British people had changed too. They believed the colonies should have the right to rule themselves. Trade with Europe, the USA and Japan was becoming more important.

Britain gave up most of the colonies without a fight and still has friendly relations with most of them.

# Consequences of the Empire

The British Empire was the biggest the world had ever known. For over 200 years it affected the lives of millions of people. Its effects are still being felt today as the diagram shows on the next page.

**Source D**  British generals surrender to the Americans

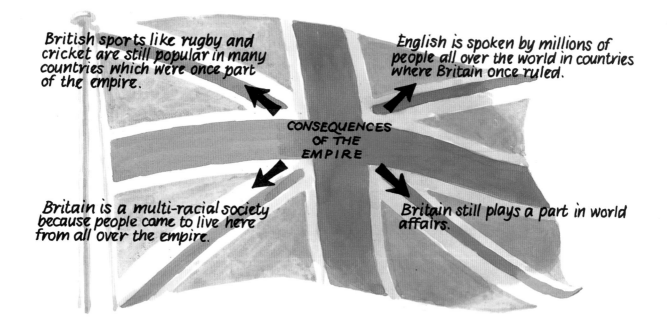

British sports like rugby and cricket are still popular in many countries which were once part of the empire.

English is spoken by millions of people all over the world in countries where Britain once ruled.

CONSEQUENCES OF THE EMPIRE

Britain is a multi-racial society because people came to live here from all over the empire.

Britain still plays a part in world affairs.

## TALKING POINTS

1 Most of the Empire countries held huge celebrations when they became independent. Why do you think they did this?

2 Britain is now a multi-racial country because of the Empire. In what ways is this a good thing? What problems does this create?

### WORKFILE

1 Make a list of all the Empire countries shown on the inside front cover map. Put them in alphabetical order. Make up a title.

2 Between 1750 and 1900 British attitudes towards the Empire changed. Copy and complete the table. Work out when the following statements might have been made. Write them in the correct column. Some may fit in both columns. Make up two more statements yourself.

a 'My slaves are lucky. I feed them regularly and treat them well.'

b 'Each country has a right to rule itself.'

c 'People should be free to trade with whom they want to.'

d 'I am proud that Britain is so powerful and rules so many countries.'

e 'India is the brightest jewel in the crown of our Empire.'

3 Draw a diagram to show the consequences of the Empire for life in Britain today.

4 Write a sentence or two about:
• the birth of the USA
• the end of slavery in the Empire

| Attitudes in | |
|---|---|
| 1750 | 1950 |
| | |
| | |

# What Was it Like Living in Britain?

## privies

Many people did badly out of the Industrial Revolution. Jobs in mines and factories were poorly paid. Many people didn't have a job at all. In the 19th century maybe ⅓ of the population did not earn enough to live on. What was life like for these people?

Use Sources A–E to answer this question. These descriptions were written by rich people who visited the poor parts of towns and cities.

**Source A**  Collecting water

**Source B**  Liverpool, 1872

"Every stairway swarms with children. Their faces are pale. The rags they wear are full of holes. They have neither shoes nor stockings. They are vilely dirty."

**Source C**  A street in Leeds, 1845

. . . there is "no form or drainage or cleansing. Garbage and filth of all kinds is thrown onto the streets. Privies are few, open to view in both front and rear. They often remain without removal of the filth for six months."

**Source D**  Inside a London home, 1873

"The walls are damp and crumbling. The ceiling is black. The floor is rotten and broken away. Wind and rain sweep in through gaps which seem everywhere. The woman, her husband and six children live, eat and sleep in this one room."

**Source E**  A poor London home, 1851

"A few sacks were thrown over a mattress filled with straw. There were no fire irons or cooking utensils. An old chest served as a chair. A board resting on a trestle did as a table. Children are fed chiefly on bread and treacle. At dinner they have boiled potatoes or cabbage smeared with fat from the bacon with which it was boiled."

**WORKFILE**

Seebohm Rowntree was one rich person who took an interest in how people lived. He paid for a study to be carried out in York his home town. Suppose you were one of his team of investigators. Use the information you have just looked at and your imagination. Fill in this report to say what you have found on one of your visits.

# Report on living conditions in the town of York commissioned by Mr Seebohm Rowntree in the year of our Lord 1899

| Name of investigator | Date of visit | Name of street | House number |
|---|---|---|---|
| Number of rooms | Name of family | Number of adults | Number of children |

**Outside appearance of street / dwelling.**

| Cooking facilities / diet of family. | Toilet / washing facilities and water supply. |
|---|---|
| Heating / Lighting | |
| Furniture | General condition of dwelling |

# 9

## *What Was it Like Working in Britain?*

**foundry, service**

Many people in the 19th century lived in very bad conditions. For most of them working conditions were not much better or were even worse.

Many people worked in factories, mines and workshops that were very dangerous. Workers became trapped in factory machines. Underground explosions in mines killed people. Many died from lung diseases caused by breathing in coal, cotton or clay dust over a number of years.

Millions of people worked on farms or 'in service' for rich people. The work was hard, backbreaking and mostly very boring. People often worked long hours. Servants began their day at 5 a.m. when they lit the fires in the house. They did not finish work until bedtime. Farm labourers were often digging in the fields from dawn to dusk. Even so they hardly earned enough money to feed their families.

Children as young as three years old worked to earn some money for the family. Most children started work when they were seven or eight years old. Boys and girls worked in all sorts of jobs.

Ellison Jack was eleven in 1842. This is how she describes her work in a coalmine.

"I have been working below ground for three years with my father. He takes me down at 2 in the morning and I come up at 2 next afternoon. I have to carry my load of coal up four ladders. My task is to fill five tubs in 20 journeys. I have had the strap when I did not do my bidding."

### WORKFILE

**1** It is 1835. Your sister's boyfriend has just been killed at work. Design a poster to warn other people in town about the dangers they face at work.

**2** Make a flowchart or a picture strip to show a day in the life of a factory worker.

**Working in a cotton mill**
This picture clearly shows how the large machines were made to work. Large belts connected the wheels on the machines to drive shafts which ran along the ceiling. The drive shafts in turn were powered by steam engines.

Many workplaces had very strict rules. Workers were fined if they did not obey. This game shows what might have happened to you if you had worked in a factory in 1850.

**You will need:**

- three or four players
- a die or numbered papers
- a blank copy of your fines record

## How to play

The game begins on Monday. Take it in turns to throw. Look at the game chart. Have you broken any rules today? Look up your offence on the list of rules. Fill in your fines record. Then go on to Tuesday.

## At the end

Add up your fines. The winner is the one with the smallest amount of fines.

### GAME CHART

|           | 1          | 2   | 3           | 4          | 5   | 6   |
|-----------|------------|-----|-------------|------------|-----|-----|
| Monday    | A 5 mins   | F   | D           | D          | ☺   | D   |
| Tuesday   | A 10 mins  | ☺   | B           | F          | E   | C   |
| Wednesday | C          | B   | A 15 mins   | C          | B   | B   |
| Thursday  | E          | F   | D           | F          | D   | ☺   |
| Friday    | C          | ☺   | ☺           | A 5 mins   | ☺   | E   |
| Saturday  | E          | F   | A 10 mins   | E          | B   | C   |

☺ = No rule broken so no fine

### FINES RECORD

|           | Offence | fine |
|-----------|---------|------|
| Monday    |         |      |
| Tuesday   |         |      |
| Wednesday |         |      |
| Thursday  |         |      |
| Friday    |         |      |
| Saturday  |         |      |
|           | Total fines |  |

### RULES TO BE OBSERVED IN THIS FACTORY

(A) Any person coming in late shall be fined as follows:    5 minutes = 2p, 10 minutes = 4p, 15 minutes = 6p.

(B) For any oil wasted or spilled on the floor.    2p fine.

(C) Any person leaving their work and found talking with other work people.    2p fine.

(D) Work people shall wash themselves at least twice a week on Mondays and Thursdays. Any found not washed will be fined 3p.

(E) Any person bringing dirty bobbins will be fined 1p.

(F) For every oath, swearing or insolent language  3p fine.

# Why Wasn't Something Done?

vote, **election, working class, revolution, guillotine**

Today everyone in Britain over the age of 18 has a say in who runs the country. Every four or five years they vote in a General Election. The people they choose are called Members of Parliament (MPs). They form the government. They rule until the next election (Source A).

Source A  Casting a vote

In 1800 Britain was run by the rich. Only rich people could vote. They voted for people who would look after their interests. Most rich people did not think they should pay higher wages to their workers.

MPs did not want to upset rich people or they would vote for someone else at the next election. The government did not worry too much about the 'working classes' who did not have a vote.

That is why for a long time nothing was done about the bad living and working conditions.

By 1800 though the rich were starting to worry. They feared a 'revolution'. A revolution had happened in France in 1789. The people arrested the king and formed their own government. Many people were beheaded on the guillotine including the king and many rich people (Source B).

Source B  The guillotine

A revolution had happened in the USA in 1776. The Americans threw out their British rulers (see page 35). The new government set out its beliefs.

We believe every citizen has a right to freely choose their government

# The Revolutionary Wars

The British ruling classes thought these were dangerous ideas. Could a revolution happen in Britain? Not if the rich could help it. Britain went to war with France. The government hoped to stop the French Revolution spreading to Britain and other countries. The bitter wars lasted for over 20 years. The French leader Napoleon was a brilliant general. His armies fought well. They won many battles.

Britain's best weapon was her navy. Admiral Nelson led his ships to victory at the Battle of Trafalgar in 1805. Britain started to get the upper hand. Napoleon was finally beaten at the Battle of Waterloo in 1815 by troops led by the Duke of Wellington (Source C).

**Source C**  The Battle of Waterloo

## Peterloo

The war did not remove the threat of revolution in Britain. There were riots and protest meetings all over the country. One meeting in 1819 became famous. At St Peter's Fields in Manchester soldiers broke up the crowd (Source D). Hundreds of unarmed people were hurt. Thirteen people died. Afterwards, in the same year, the government passed harsh laws to stop more protests.

In the end a revolution did happen. It did not happen in one place or at any one time. All through the 19th century ordinary people fought to improve their lives. They demanded a bigger say in what was going on. Things did improve. In some ways this revolution is still happening today.

**Source D**  The Massacre at St Peter's Fields

## TALKING POINTS

1 Look at Sources C and D. In what ways are the events shown here similar? In what ways are they different?

2 'Peterloo' was what the government's opponents called the St Peter's Field Massacre. Why do you think they gave it that name?

# 11

# *The Reformers*

**reform, conflict, petitions, trade unions, strike**

In the 19th century there were many people who wanted to 'reform' or change things. They wanted to make Britain a fairer place for more people. There were different groups of reformers. They worked in different ways and had different aims. Some reformers wanted better working conditions. Some reformers wanted to change the way the government was chosen. For many working people the issue was simple. They were fighting for better wages and enough food to eat.

Getting things changed was not easy. Some people were afraid of change as we saw on page 41. Many richer people were happy with things the way they were. They felt threatened. The fight for reform caused many conflicts in the 19th century. The following picture strips tell of three different groups of people who fought for change.

## TALKING POINTS

1 Write down three things about life in Britain today which you would like to change. What would you like to happen? What could you do to bring about these changes?

2 Write down three things about life in Britain today which you don't want to change. What could you do to keep things from changing?

## *The Chartists*

Chartists wanted to change the way the government was chosen. They set out their aims in 'The People's Charter'. Their main demand was that all men over the age of 21 should have the vote. They took petitions to Parliament in 1839, 1842 and again in 1848.

3

4

5

## WORKFILE

**1** The pictures are in the right order. Try to work out what is happening in each picture. Match the captions below with the correct picture. Copy this table. Write in the caption letter for each picture.

| Picture Number | 1 | 2 | 3 | 4 | 5 |
|---|---|---|---|---|---|
| Caption Letter | | | | | |

**A** 1848. Feargus O'Connor, the Chartist leader, calls for a new petition. Six million signatures are collected.

**B** The government fears a revolution and prepares for trouble. Eight thousand soldiers are brought in to protect Parliament under the command of the Duke of Wellington.

**C** A grand march is planned to take the petition to Parliament. Half a million people are expected to meet at the start on Kennington Common, London.

**D** The government rejects the Chartist's demands. The petition is thrown out. Some Chartists are arrested. No more petitions are ever organised.

**E** The great meeting does not happen. Far less people than expected turn up. The march is cancelled and the petition is carried to Parliament in taxi cabs. The Chartists are made to look foolish.

**2** Use the pictures and captions to help you write your own account of the Chartists. Say
- what they wanted
- what they did to get their way
- how successful you think they were

**3** Write an account of the factory reformers and trade unions using the pictures and captions which follow.

# Trade Unions

Some workers formed trade unions. They aimed to try to improve their pay and working conditions. They went on strike to get what they wanted.

Sometimes they won. Sometimes they were forced back to work by a lack of money. Many trade unions were formed in the 19th century. One strike by some of Britain's poorest workers became famous.

A reporter interviews women who work in a match factory in London. Her report describes shocking conditions in the Bryant & May factory

The factory owners deny the report is true. The women who spoke to the reporter are sacked.

The reporter, Annie Besant, helps the workers to form a trade union.

The workers demand better conditions and go on strike until the owners agree.

Most members of the public are on the women's side. After three weeks the owners agree to the women's demands. They go back to work having won a famous victory.

# Factory Reformers

Many people, both rich and poor, worked to
improve factory conditions. They held meetings
and wrote to newspapers. They hoped to
persuade MPs. They wanted new laws to cut
working hours and make workplaces safer.

1830. The Leeds Mercury publishes a letter
written by Richard Oastler. He describes working
conditions in some Yorkshire factories. Many
people are shocked. Oastler starts a campaign
to get things improved.

1833. One M.P. Lord Shaftesbury, calls for a law to
stop people working more than 10 hours in one day.
M.P.s vote on this idea but reject it.

1833 Parliament discusses working
hours in factories. They listen to the views
of some factory owners. They say any
change will cost them money.

Shaftesbury and others keep up
the campaign. They visit factories to
collect evidence which they use to
persuade Parliament to act.

Some M.P.s are persuaded to change
their opinion. Parliament makes several
new laws to control working hours
and conditions in factories.

## WORKFILE

Use the information you have just read to complete the chart below.

1 Fill in the missing words in the boxes. Use these words:

meetings    by    British    Nelson    the    Duke    new    government    and

2 Cut out the boxes and stick them in the right place on the chart. Use the dates to help you work out where they go.

| **North America.** American Revolution throws out _ _ _ _ _ rulers and sets up a people's _ _ _ _ _. | **Manchester, England.** Soldiers kill protesters at _ _ _ _ _ 'Peterloo' massacre. | **Paris, France.** French Revolution begins. The king _ _ _ _ _ many nobles are guillotined. |
|---|---|---|
| **Battle of Waterloo.** Napoleon is defeated _ _ _ _ _ British and German forces led by the _ _ _ _ _ of Wellington. | **Battle of Trafalgar.** British fleet led by Admiral _ _ _ _ _ defeats the French. | **London, England.** British government passes strict _ _ _ _ _ laws to stop riots and protest _ _ _ _ _. |

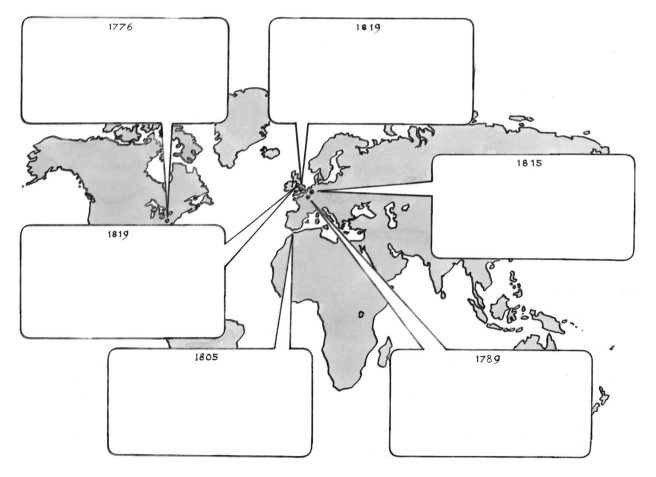

# Glossary

**aristocrats** – highest ranking group of people in wealth and importance. Usually have a title given to them by the king or queen eg duke, duchess

**bale** – bundle of goods

**bankrupt** – person who has to stop trading because he or she has no money

**barrel** – large wooden cylinder used for carrying liquids

**business** – doing something to make money eg making or trading goods

**canal** – a man-made waterway

**colony** – an area of land taken over by people from another part of the world

**competition** – people trying to do better than one another eg in sport or business

**conflict** – fighting. Serious argument or disagreement

**conservatory** – glass building attached to a house

**culture** – distinctive way of life

**decrease** – to become less

**election** – the time when people choose who should represent them

**emperor** – the leader of an empire

**empire** – a large area of the world, usually containing several countries, ruled by one government

**energy** – power

**estate** – an area of land usually owned by one rich family. Might include several farms and villages

**expedition** – a long journey, often with a purpose such as discovering new places

**exploit** – to make unfair use of something or somebody

**export** – to send goods abroad for trade

**factory** – a place where things are made on a large scale

**foundry** – a place where iron is melted and cast into shapes

**guillotine** – a machine used in the French Revolution for chopping people's heads off

**handloom** – hand powered machine used for weaving cloth

**import** – to bring goods into the country for trade

**increase** – to become bigger

**independent** – free to choose for themselves

**Industrial Revolution** – period of history when industries and factories replaced farming as the main form of business in Britain

**industry** – manufacturing or making things

**iron** – a strong, heavy type of metal

**material** – substances from which things are made eg iron, cloth, wood

**mechanical** – something which is made or worked by machine

**merchant** – a person who buys and sells goods with the aim of making money

**native** – born to one particular place

**petition** – a paper signed by many people, usually with the aim of persuading someone to do something

**population** – the total number of people living in a particular area

**power** – the ability to get something to move or to happen

**privy** – a basic toilet, often just a bar to sit on

**profit** – to gain an amount of money

**reform** – to change things

**regiment** – a group of soldiers

**revolution** – a large-scale change

**sepoy** – an Indian soldier working for the East India Company

**service** – working as a servant for rich people

**slave** – a person who is owned by another person and has to do what they say

**spinning** – making raw wool or cotton into thread

**statistics** – information collected in the form of numbers

**strike** – refusing to work with the aim of trying to force an employer to do something eg to pay you more wages

**Trade Union** – an organisation formed when workers join together to try to improve their pay or working conditions

**transport** – means of moving people or goods

**viceroy** – king's or queen's representative who rules another part of the world on their behalf

**warehouse** – a place where goods are stored before being bought or sold

**weaving** – the process of making thread into cloth

**working class** – the social group which forms part of the population which earns a living by manual labour